COMMUNITY HELPERS

Pilots

by Kate Moening

BELLWETHER MEDIA • MINNEAPOLIS, MN

Note to Librarians, Teachers, and Parents:

Blastoff! Readers are carefully developed by literacy experts and combine standards-based content with developmentally appropriate text.

Level 1 provides the most support through repetition of high-frequency words, light text, predictable sentence patterns, and strong visual support.

Level 2 offers early readers a bit more challenge through varied simple sentences, increased text load, and less repetition of high-frequency words.

Level 3 advances early-fluent readers toward fluency through increased text and concept load, less reliance on visuals, longer sentences, and more literary language.

Level 4 builds reading stamina by providing more text per page, increased use of punctuation, greater variation in sentence patterns, and increasingly challenging vocabulary.

Level 5 encourages children to move from "learning to read" to "reading to learn" by providing even more text, varied writing styles, and less familiar topics.

Whichever book is right for your reader, Blastoff! Readers are the perfect books to build confidence and encourage a love of reading that will last a lifetime!

This edition first published in 2019 by Bellwether Media, Inc.

No part of this publication may be reproduced in whole or in part without written permission of the publisher. For information regarding permission, write to Bellwether Media, Inc., Attention: Permissions Department, 6012 Blue Circle Drive, Minnetonka, MN 55343.

Library of Congress Cataloging-in-Publication Data

LC record for Pilots available at https://lccn.loc.gov/ 2018030406

Text copyright © 2019 by Bellwether Media, Inc. BLASTOFF! READERS and associated logos are trademarks and/or registered trademarks of Bellwether Media, Inc. SCHOLASTIC, CHILDREN'S PRESS, and associated logos are trademarks and/or registered trademarks of Scholastic Inc., 557 Broadway, New York, NY 10012.

Editor: Betsy Rathburn   Designer: Brittany McIntosh

Printed in the United States of America, North Mankato, MN.

Table of Contents

Ready for Takeoff

The pilot boards the airplane. She reads the airplane controls.

Next, she radios **air traffic control**. The **runway** is clear. Time to fly!

What Are Pilots?

Pilots fly aircraft such as helicopters and airplanes. They keep people safe in the air!

Some pilots fly aircraft that carry **passengers**. Others **transport** goods such as mail.

passengers

What Do Pilots Do?

Pilots make sure the aircraft is safe before they fly. Sometimes, a **crew** helps.

**crew
member**

Pilots tell air traffic control the path they will take. This also keeps the aircraft safe.

radio

sunglasses

compass

speedometer

air traffic
control

Weather changes quickly! Pilots fly through rain, snow, or sunshine.

What Makes a Good Pilot?

Special tools help pilots **navigate**. Pilots must learn to use each tool.

Pilot Skills

- ✓ good communicators
- ✓ alert
- ✓ good with machines
- ✓ careful

navigation
tools

Takeoffs and landings can be tricky. Pilots are careful to keep passengers safe!

Glossary

air traffic control

people on the ground who help pilots take off and land aircraft

passengers

people traveling in an aircraft

crew

people who help pilots keep aircraft clean and safe

runway

an open road where pilots drive aircraft to take off and land

navigate

to control or direct a trip

transport

to carry from one place to another

To Learn More

AT THE LIBRARY

Reinke, Beth Bence. *Helicopters on the Go*. Minneapolis, Minn.: Lerner Publications, 2018.

Schuh, Mari. *Bus Drivers*. Minneapolis, Minn.: Bellwether Media, 2018.

Thomas, Isabel. *Amelia Earhart: Little Guides to Great Lives*. London, U.K.: Laurence King Publishing, 2018.

ON THE WEB

FACTSURFER

Factsurfer.com gives you a safe, fun way to find more information.

1. Go to www.factsurfer.com.

2. Enter "pilots" into the search box.

3. Click the "Surf" button and select your book cover to see a list of related web sites.

Index

The images in this book are reproduced through the courtesy of: michaeljung, front cover; Angelo Giampiccolo, pp. 4-5; motive56, pp. 6-7; Digital Vision/ Getty Images, pp. 8-9; TunedIn by Westend61, pp. 10-11; Wim Wiskerke/ Alamy, pp. 14-15; Cultura RM/ Alamy, pp. 14-15; Teamdaddy, p. 15 (radio); ltummy, p. 15 (sunglasses); Ensuper, p. 15 (compass); Jeffrey B. Banke, p. 15 (speedometer); moto, pp. 16-17; Skycolors, pp. 18-19, 20-21, 22 (bottom left); Burben, p. 22 (top left); Sorbis, p. 22 (middle left); Patryk Kosmider, p. 22 (top right); Cariad Eccleston, p. 22 (middle right); Stas Volik, p. 22 (bottom right).